This book is to be returned or t
the las

Disasters *in* Nature

Tornadoes

Catherine Chambers

Heinemann
LIBRARY

www.heinemann.co.uk
Visit our website to find out more information about Heinemann Library books.

To order:
☎ Phone 44 (0) 1865 888066
▤ Send a fax to 44 (0) 1865 314091
▯ Visit the Heinemann Bookshop at www.heinemann.co.uk to browse our catalogue and order online.

First published in Great Britain by Heinemann Library, Halley Court, Jordan Hill, Oxford OX2 8EJ a division of Reed Educational and Professional Publishing Ltd. Heinemann is a registered trademark of Reed Educational & Professional Publishing Ltd.

OXFORD MELBOURNE AUCKLAND JOHANNESBURG BLANTYRE
GABORONE IBADAN PORTSMOUTH (NH) USA CHICAGO

© Reed Educational and Professional Publishing Ltd 2000
The moral right of the proprietor has been asserted.

Designed by Celia Floyd
Originated by Dot Gradations
Printed by Wing King Tong in Hong Kong

04 03 02 01 00
10 9 8 7 6 5 4 3 2 1

ISBN 0 431 09602 3

British Library Cataloguing in Publication Data

Chambers, Catherine
Tornado. – (Disasters in Nature)
1. Tornadoes – Juvenile literature
I. Title
551.5'53

Acknowledgements

The Publishers would like to thank the following for permission to reproduce photographs:

Bruce Coleman Collection: Andrew Davies pg.43, RIM Campbell pg.21; *Camera Press*: pg.36; *Colorific*: Jose Azel/Aurora pg.29; *FLPA*: David T Crewcock pg.41, H Hoflinger pg.20, R Jennings pg.18, Robert Steinau pg.26; *Hulton Getty*: pg.8, pg.33; *Image Bank*: GSO Images pg.16; *Link Picture Library*: Jeroen Snijdera pg.12; *Network*: Alan Dietrich/Saba pg.29; *NHPA*: Andy Rouse pg.39; *NOAA*: NSSL Picture Collection pg.7, pg.34; *Panos*: Fred Hoogervorst pg.10, pg.44; *Photri*: pg31; *Planet Earth Pictures*: Mary Clay pg.11; *Popperfoto*: George Frey pg.37, Reuters pg.30; *Rex Features*: pg.45; *Science Photo Library*: Larry Miller pg.14, National Centre for Atmospheric Research USA pg.19; *Superstock*: pg.4.

Cover photograph reproduced with permission of Liaison International.

Our thanks to Mandy Barker for her comments in the preparation of this book.

Every effort has been made to contact copyright holders of any material reproduced in this book. Any omissions will be rectified in subsequent printings if notice is given to the Publisher.

Any words appearing in the text in bold, **like this**, are explained in the Glossary.

Contents

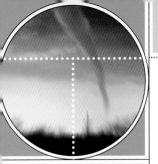

What is a tornado?

Tornadoes – violent, dark grey, twisting, sucking winds – are a mystery. When they occur, people can see them and observe their effects, but no one is sure exactly how tornadoes form. Tornadoes, or **twisters** as they are also known, rotate around a **funnel** of very **low pressure**. They begin inside deep thunderclouds and appear to hang from them in an upside-down cone shape.

The tornado's funnel may be quite narrow – no more than 100 metres (330 feet) across – or it may be as much as 1.5 kilometres (about 1 mile). The tornado's **path** may be as short as a few kilometres – or it might run for 750 kilometres (over 450 miles)!

Where do tornadoes happen?

The United States of America (US) suffers more damaging tornadoes than any other country in the world – often 1000 or more in a year. The area of the US most commonly hit by tornadoes has been called **Tornado Alley**. Australia, Canada, parts of Russia, central Asia, Japan, Italy and the UK are also hit by tornadoes.

This tornado looks too narrow to harm anything in its way, but it is powerful enough to suck up tree trunks, roofs and solid walls along its path.

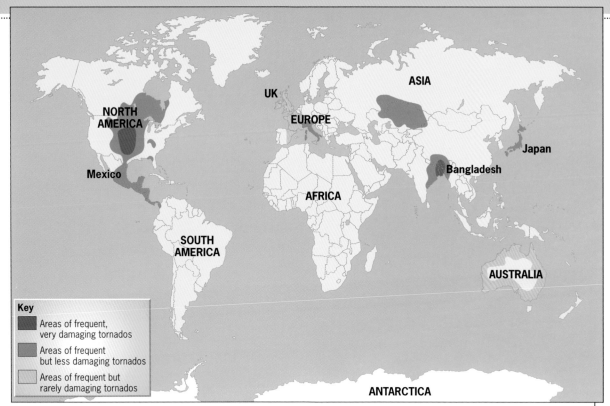

Key
- Areas of frequent, very damaging tornados
- Areas of frequent but less damaging tornados
- Areas of frequent but rarely damaging tornados

Tornadoes in our hands

Modern methods of predicting tornadoes and tracking them have meant that warnings can be given earlier than they used to be, but it does seem that the strength and frequency of tornadoes have increased. This is thought to be possibly due to **global warming**. Tornadoes are increasingly turning into disasters because of the growing numbers of people who have to live in tornado paths.

Tornadoes on our minds

Have tornadoes really got worse or do we just hear more about them and more about the devastation that they can cause? Through satellite communication, all over the world people can sit in their own homes and watch and listen to the disaster as it unfolds. More and more people read newspapers, but why do some tornadoes make the news headlines while others are ignored?

Tornado disasters occur regularly in all these areas shown, but are most frequently damaging in the United States of America.

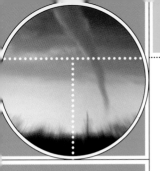

'Terrible Tuesday' – a tornado disaster

On Tuesday 10 April 1979 a column of dark grey cloud blackened the sky to the south of Wichita Falls city in the US state of Texas. The people were used to such sights, for they lived in **Tornado Alley**, a track running from the Gulf of Mexico to the Great Lakes. But nothing had ever prepared them for something quite so huge as the tornado that was about to hit them.

The Wichita Falls disaster

The **twister** was 1.6 kilometres (1 mile) wide, travelled 13 kilometres (8 miles), and tore a bare strip through the city. This single, monstrous tornado ripped apart a large community within a very short time. Forty-five people died and 1700 were injured. Three thousand homes were completely flattened, 2000 were damaged and 20 000 people were left with nowhere to live. By the final count, over 20 per cent of the city's buildings were destroyed or were declared unsafe to use.

The warm air from the south not only rises as it meets the cold bands of air from the north and west. It also climbs steadily all the way from the coast. This means that the moisture in the air is gradually cooling and **condensing** slightly all the time, creating **instability**.

How did it happen?

Wichita Falls lies to the east of the Rocky Mountains, on the northern border of the state of Texas. Here, on the Great Plains, the tornado season reaches its peak between April and May. Bands of cold air come down in waves from the north and north-west of America. The bands meet a **jet stream** of more cold, dry air coming from the west. These are joined by very warm, moist and unstable bands of air moving northwards from the Gulf of Mexico. When the warm moist air meets the cold, dry air, it has to climb above it. As each wave of warm air rises the moisture in it begins to condense, forming lines of thunderclouds, providing ideal conditions for tornadoes.

Impact!

The people of Wichita were given very little warning that a terrifying tornado was approaching. For many people, there was no time to escape. Some were lucky enough to have a basement to hide in. Others hid under the stairs, in cupboards, the bath and even a cheese vault. Outside, many stayed in their cars, believing this was the safest thing to do, but over half of the deaths occurred when the cars were sucked up, tossed into the air and then thrown onto the ground.

The scale of devastation at Wichita Falls was huge.

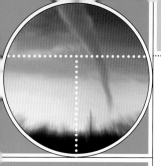

Moving on

10 April 1999 was the twentieth anniversary of the Wichita Falls tornado disaster. People all over the city remembered the dead and relived the destruction, but they also recalled with pride how they coped and supported each other, and how the city has renewed itself since then.

More than this, the disaster became a turning point in American disaster history, which has enabled other communities to be better prepared in the face of a tornado. The improvements in predicting and managing tornadoes have been put to good use. Their success was made clear in the Oklahoma tornado disaster in May 1999. Sadly, people still died and there was a lot of destruction, as we shall see on page 11. But without Wichita, it could have been a lot worse.

In the aftermath of the disaster, buildings that were destroyed were covered with flat concrete slabs, rather like tombstones. Most have now been built on but some remain as a cold reminder of 'Terrible Tuesday'.

Lessons learned

There were many lessons to be learned, not just for this city, but for all American communities lying in the **path** of tornadoes. The technique for measuring tornadoes, known as **Doppler radar**, had only been in action for two years (see page 31). Research into its use was patchy and underfunded but, after the Wichita disaster, predicting and preparing for tornadoes had suddenly become an important project in the eyes of most Americans. The national Doppler radar system had top priority and money for its development became immediately available. Now a **Doppler dome** stands outside Wichita Falls – a symbol of comfort but a reminder of sad times, too.

Safety first

During the tornado, many people were saved because they quickly found their way to tornado shelters. The disaster proved how important these shelters were, and more were built or provided in the city. Building regulations were not changed but building contractors began to include concrete storm shelters inside new homes as standard. This was so that people did not have to put themselves in danger by fleeing outside to public shelters.

Advice on building a safe room inside older dwellings was also made widely available. The Internet makes sure that instructions reach an even wider audience today. Internet websites even describe how to build a basic tornado shelter. The family tornado shelter is usually a simple cupboard, made stronger with a steel frame, double walls and extra studs. More importantly, people are made aware that seeking a proper shelter is the first priority. Videos of the Wichita disaster are used as a teaching tool throughout **Tornado Alley**, to show the importance of taking notice of warnings.

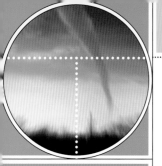

Hitting the headlines

The Wichita Falls tornado is a very well-documented natural disaster, so people know a lot about it. The disaster hit the newspaper headlines for many days in the United States, and its devastating images filled the television screens. Far across the oceans the tornado was a top priority for many European broadcasting networks and newspapers.

All this attention was due partly to the scale of the death and damage, but it was also helped by the huge number of news networks in the United States and the ability of news reporters to travel quickly from one state to another. Added to this, the United States had in place the resources and technology to produce facts and figures quickly – the approximate strength, width and speed of the storm, the amount of devastation and roughly how much it would cost to put right.

On 2 April 1977 the deadliest cluster of tornadoes ever recorded struck Bangladesh. Nine hundred people were killed and 6000 were injured. Yet there was not the same amount of international media coverage as there was for the Wichita Falls disaster. Few international news reporters cover stories on a regular basis in Bangladesh. Once there, they often find **communications** and transport difficult and many reporters have to rely on aid agencies and translators for information.

Bangladesh was hit by the deadliest group of tornadoes ever recorded in 1977.

The modern media

Nowadays, tornado technology is more accurate than it was 20 years ago. News reporters and amateur tornado trackers know when a really big tornado is coming and they film the **twister** as it approaches. They are on the spot when it strikes and can transmit images of devastation around the world in a very short time. This was made clear on 3 May 1999, when a series of tornadoes whirled towards Oklahoma City in the US – one of them 1.6 kilometres (1 mile) wide. Forty-five people died, thousands of buildings were flattened and whole suburbs were destroyed. Over the next few days the tornadoes continued their devastating journey over 240 kilometres (150 miles) northward, causing more havoc. At this time in Europe, the war in Kosovo, in the former Yugoslavia, was top priority for news networks but on 3 May the war shared headline space with the Oklahoma tornadoes. In the United States, they dominated the headlines for several days.

We hear very little about tornadoes in Mexico, and yet it suffers from them every year. Unlike the United States, Mexico does not have the resources to track and measure tornadoes. Tropical storms, like this one, are the perfect breeding ground for tornadoes.

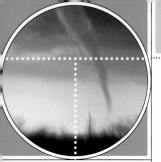

The world's weather

Tornadoes hang from deep, dark thunderclouds, heavy with rain and hail. Without these, tornadoes would never form. The moisture carried in the cloud is part of the **water cycle**. The water cycle is the way in which the earth's supply of water is recycled all the time, in different forms. Sometimes it is held in the air as invisible **water vapour** or as tiny droplets in wispy cloud. At other times it falls as rain, sleet, snow or hail, but most of it lies in massive oceans, seas and lakes. It flows in rivers and streams – or it lies frozen in ice-sheets and glaciers. There is always the same amount of water on the earth.

What happens to the water?

When the sun shines and the wind blows over large masses of water, the water heats up and molecules escape from the surface to form a vapour, which is a gas. This means that some water has **evaporated** into the air. If the air is warm, it holds more moisture than if it was cold. The warm air rises, carrying the water vapour with it. As the warm, moist air rises it cools and the water vapour **condenses** into tiny droplets which form clouds. As the clouds rise even higher, the droplets become **super-cooled**, icy and even larger as more water vapour condenses. These droplets are heavier, too, and fall as rain.

Warm, moist air can carry, and then drop, enormous quantities of water.

A lot of this rain falls on the oceans, but some falls on land. Clouds rise up hill and mountain slopes, shedding rain before they reach the other side. Sometimes when banks of warm, moist air meet blocks of **high pressure** they cannot move along, only upwards, where the air cools rapidly. If the air is very moist then a lot of condensation occurs and torrential rain follows.

Tornadoes begin to form at the base of very heavy stormclouds, so without the water cycle there would be no tornadoes at all. The water cycle is a very fast global system, which makes it very difficult to predict perfectly. Tornadoes are part of this unpredictable system and are no easier to cope with than any other weather disaster, such as flood, drought or **hurricane**.

What makes the wind blow?

Wind is caused by air moving from areas of high pressure (masses of cool, dense air) to areas of **low pressure** (masses of warm, light, rising air). This exchange of air masses can be quite gentle – just a faint breeze might blow. But if there is an area of very low pressure, caused by a lot of warm air rising, then air from the high pressure area rushes in fast, in the form of winds, to take its place. This rush of wind is what makes a tornado so strong, as air swoops in to replace the air sucked up into the **funnel**. This is just one feature of tornadoes. There are others.

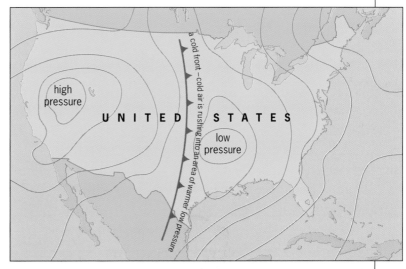

This diagram shows where an area of low pressure meets an area of high pressure. This meeting place is called a front.

13

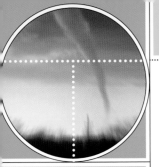

What makes a tornado?

Tornadoes are towering, spinning **funnels** of wind and cloud. They can reach 1000 metres (about 3300 feet) up into the sky and the air inside them can spin at up to 480 kilometres per hour (about 300 miles per hour). The pressure inside the funnel is so low it is like a **vacuum** that sucks up everything that it touches. But how do tornadoes form?

This funnel is not yet a true tornado, as it has not touched down. Sometimes, the funnels never reach **touchdown** point.

Tornado types

- Some tornadoes consist of several funnels – a large, central funnel with smaller ones spinning around it. These can form inside the wall of the central funnel. Usually, there are from two to five small ones which can disappear and reform later.

- Some tornadoes are invisible because no cloud forms in the funnel. The only evidence for them is the dust and objects thrown up in their path.

- Tornadoes are sometimes invisible because they are masked by cloud. In Missouri in 1925, a rolling cloud, low down on the ground, hid a huge tornado behind it.

1 Cumulonimbus clouds (thunderclouds) form as warm, moist air rises into cold air.

2 A fast, horizontal wind blows against the clouds, at a constant angle.

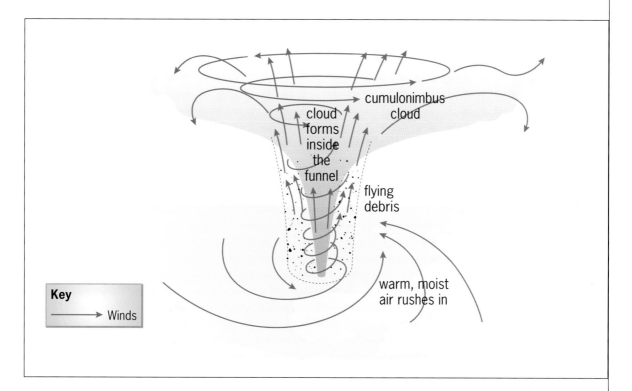

cumulonimbus cloud

cloud forms inside the funnel

flying debris

warm, moist air rushes in

Key
→ Winds

3 As the wind blows, warm air gets sucked right up to the top of the thundercloud and the vertical twisting motion begins. The spin is caused by the angles at which the different winds blow, at different **altitudes** and acting at different speeds. The spinning wind then dips down below the cloud, sucking up warm air beneath it. Air rushes in at the bottom, to replace the warm, rising air. It also rushes in at the top, where more warm air lies, sucking air up faster through the funnel as it does so.

4 As the column lengthens, **water vapour** inside it **condenses** and dark clouds rise up through the funnel. They condense further quite low down and release more heat – fuelling the tornado. If the whirling wind is really strong, the base of the funnel will touch the ground, and this is when the damage is done.

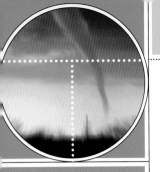

On the heels of the hurricane

Tornadoes often follow closely after a **hurricane**. They form as the hurricane rushes inland, and they usually travel along on the right-hand side of it. Sometimes there are only a few, and usually no more than ten, but in 1967 Texas was battered by 115 tornadoes that ran alongside Hurricane Beulah.

How do hurricanes happen?

A hurricane is a fierce whirling wind that blows in an inward spiral, from an area of **high pressure** to an area of very **low pressure**. Hurricanes form as great masses of very warm, moist air rise, reducing air pressure over the oceans. These areas of very low pressure form the centre, around which the warm air rises in a whirling, upward spiral. As it does so, cooler air from an area of high pressure rushes into the space created at its base.

The **eye** forms when a hurricane reaches its peak. The eye is a wide column of calm, descending air right in the middle of the warm spiral of rising air that is wrapped around it. Once the eye has passed, the hurricane wall on the other side of it causes further devastation.

The rising air cools as it goes up and the moisture in the air **condenses**, forming banks of very heavy, lowlying, dark raincloud. The continual formation of cloud, and the rolling thunderstorms also release heat into the air, which fuels the whirling hurricane even more. The upward-turning spiral and the downward-rushing air move faster and faster as they approach land. The sea provides very little resistance to it but, once the hurricane begins to move over the land, there is no more warm moisture to pick up – so the 'fuel' runs out. There is also more friction with land and vegetation than there is with water. This friction slows up the wind and the hurricane gradually dies, but not before the storm clouds have provided ideal conditions for tornado formation.

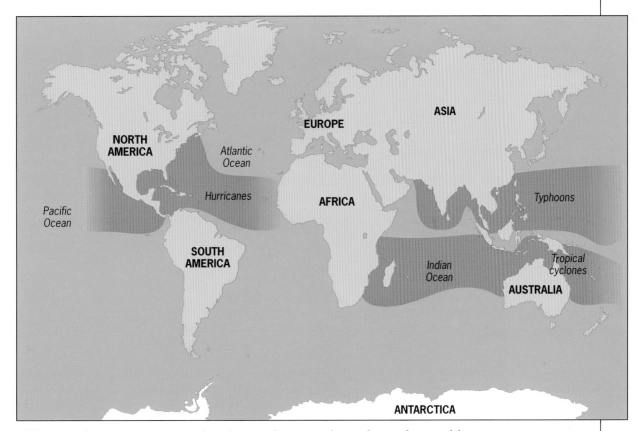

This map shows where most hurricanes happen throughout the world. Comparing it with the map on page 5, notice that tornadoes occur in many hurricane-prone areas. The concentration of tornadoes is mostly in the Atlantic Basin, whereas hurricanes are more evenly spread throughout the hotspots.

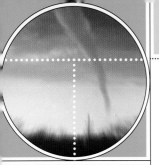

Thunder, lightning and heavy hail

Heavy thunderclouds, lightning and hailstones are often the first signs of a tornado. Sometimes they actually accompany the tornado as it whirls along. Scientists believe that hailstones and cold, downward-rushing air help to make **convection currents**. These are the movements of warm and cold air that are spun into a **vortex** – or whirling **funnel** of air – by a steady wind high up.

Tornadoes bring strange electrical storms. Flashing lights and **ball lightning** can explode like bombs among the dark clouds.

Lightning strikes

Lightning forms in thick, dark **cumulonimbus** cloud, just like tornadoes do. Inside the cloud the movement of water and ice particles create a huge **electrical charge** – positive at the top of the cloud, and negative at the bottom. The difference between the positive and negative charges can be so great that a huge spark jumps across the air between them. For a fraction of a second, along the path of the spark, the heat rises to thousands of degrees Celsius. This is seen as a lightning flash, and it is heard as an explosive noise – thunder.

How does hail happen?

Hail is yet another weather phenomenon that forms in heavy, dark cumulonimbus clouds. The clouds need to be very tall, reaching up to **altitudes** where the temperature is below zero. There the **super-cooled** water droplets are thrust even higher by strong updraughts of wind. At very high altitudes, the droplets freeze into ice. These tiny pieces of ice then stick together when they touch, and form hailstones. When the hailstones are large enough, or when the updraughts weaken, they fall as a hailstorm.

You can see from this description how tornadoes, with their strong upward movement of air, help to make very large hailstones which pelt towards the ground as the tornado rushes along.

As small hailstones rise to the top of the clouds, they get covered with layers of moisture which freeze as they rise even higher. As you can see from this picture, they look like the layers of an onion or tree trunk rings.

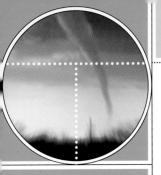

Waterspouts and dust devils

Whirling water

When a tornado forms and moves over water it sucks the water up and sprays it around the base of the **funnel**. This is known as a **waterspout**. It can completely empty a pond – and everything in it. Fish, water plants and even alligators can get sucked up and thrown aside. At the base of the funnel, the winds whip the water into waves and spray.

Most waterspouts occur in the Gulf of Mexico, the Bahamas, the west coast of Africa and in the US state of Florida. The highest number occur off the Florida Keys – a chain of islands and reefs 360 kilometres (225 miles) long, broken by channels and bays of water.

Waterspouts appear as dark tubes of water streaming from the base of a cloud. This is because the funnels are full of water droplets that are sucked up and then fall back down again.

Funnels of dust

Dust devils (also called **whirlwinds**) are like miniature tornadoes that form over very hot, dry areas, especially desert and semi-desert. Unlike tornadoes, they are not usually associated with clouds. They can often occur under clear, blue skies and they begin from the ground, not from winds at high **altitudes**.

Like tornadoes they are fed by warm air – in this case the heat **radiating** from the ground as the sun beats down on it. The winds can blow both clockwise and anticlockwise into the dust devil, wherever they occur in the world.

These whirlwinds travel mostly through very remote desert areas, such as the Sahara in West Africa. They can be small wisps of dust that swirl for just a few minutes or they can be spinning dust storms that race across the desert for hours. Dust devils are also found in the deserts of Australia, India, the Middle East and the United States – and on dry, sandy beaches!

This dust devil is whirling its way across the Sahara.

Tornado types

- Small dust devils rarely reach F0 on the **Fujita-Pearson** Scale (see page 27) but waterspouts can be as fierce as F3.

- The biggest waterspout measured so far hit the US state of Massachusetts on 19 August 1896. It was a triangular shape about 1000 metres (about 3300 feet) high. The spray spread out for 200 metres (about 650 feet) around the waterspout's tip.

- One of the biggest whirlwinds recorded spun its way over the dry saltlands of Utah in the United States. It was 750 metres (about 2500 feet) high and ran for 65 kilometres (40 miles).

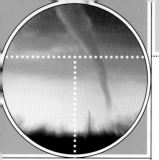

Global warming

It seems that, with each decade, an increasing number of tornadoes carve their destructive paths across the land. Clusters of tornadoes seem more frequent. Single tornadoes appear to be wider and stronger. Why is this so? Maybe it is just because we receive far more information about disasters across the world – or perhaps it is because we are able to measure tornado disasters more accurately. Or it could be that our **climate** is changing, genuinely making tornadoes more frequent and more damaging.

It takes a difference of only 1–2° Celsius (2–4° Fahrenheit) to make a change to the Earth's climate and weather patterns. We know this from the cooling effect that huge **volcanic** explosions have upon the Earth. When hot ashes and gas rise into the **stratosphere**, average world temperatures are reduced by about 1° Celsius (2° Fahrenheit). Most scientists agree that the world's climate is getting warmer. The trend shows that the Earth is probably going to heat up by 1° Celsius (2° Fahrenheit) in the next 30 years. Scientists call this rise in temperature **global warming**. How does this happen?

Living under glass

The **greenhouse effect** is thought to be partly responsible for global warming. It is caused by certain gases, particularly carbon dioxide, rising from the Earth into the **atmosphere**. Heat from the Sun is absorbed by the Earth and some is reflected and **radiated** back. These gases form a layer which acts like a huge mirror, reflecting this radiated heat back down to Earth and warming both the sea and the land. Warmer land could mean an increase in fuel for a twisting tornado. However, it is thought that the greenhouse effect is not acting on its own to cause global warming.

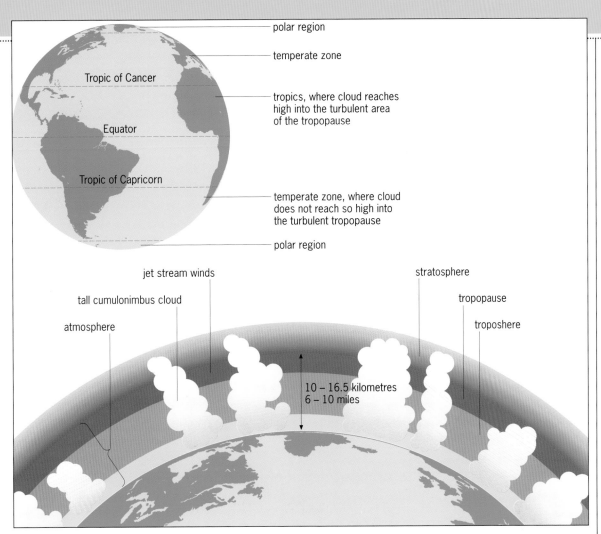

polar region

temperate zone

Tropic of Cancer

tropics, where cloud reaches high into the turbulent area of the tropopause

Equator

Tropic of Capricorn

temperate zone, where cloud does not reach so high into the turbulent tropopause

polar region

jet stream winds

stratosphere

tall cumulonimbus cloud

tropopause

atmosphere

troposhere

10 – 16.5 kilometres
6 – 10 miles

A hole in the sky

Earth is surrounded by layers of gases known as the atmosphere. This is like a blanket, stopping the full strength of the sun from reaching the Earth and filtering harmful **ultra-violet rays**. One of the most effective protective gases is **ozone**, which forms a layer in the stratosphere, between 10 and 50 kilometres (about 6–30 miles) above the Earth's surface. In recent years, the layer of ozone has become thinner, especially over Antarctica. This means that more **radiation** from the Sun is getting through. Some of this is absorbed by the land and the oceans, but some is reflected from the Earth's surface, heating the air above it, with the same result as the greenhouse effect.

Global warming causes the **troposphere** (the layer of atmosphere closest to the Earth) to heat up. The contrast in temperatures creates more winds and **turbulent** storms and could affect the number and strength of tornadoes.

23

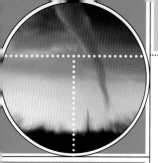

The effects of El Niño

When particularly bad climatic disasters occur, some scientists blame it on **El Niño**. This strange phenomenon causes **prevailing winds** to change direction and cool ocean currents to warm up. Over the years the effects of El Niño seem to have become more violent, causing torrential rain and heavy flooding, severe drought, dust storms and forest fires. What impact does El Niño have upon tornadoes?

The good and the bad

El Niño does not cause natural disaster everywhere. But in some parts of the world, such as Bangladesh, its effects do increase **hurricanes**, with tornadoes spinning alongside them.

In normal El Niño years, though, the Atlantic Basin suffers less destruction than usual. The bands of cold air that sweep down from Canada help to create the **turbulence** needed for tornadoes to form on the Great Plains of the United States. This air is known as the polar **jet stream**. In an El Niño year, the polar jet stream remains over Canada so the turbulence further south is reduced and there are fewer, weaker tornadoes. Added to this, stronger tropical winds high up blow away or weaken **depressions** (areas of very **low pressure**) making their way to the Atlantic Basin. This reduces the amount and strength of hurricanes and tornadoes.

Sadly, the peace does not last. Sometimes El Niño is followed by **La Niña** – a severe reversal of El Niño, and one that changes the luck of people living in **Tornado Alley**. La Niña is the complete opposite. The high tropical winds blowing eastward are weaker, and westward trade winds are stronger, making the hurricanes more forceful as they hit the coast, and the tornadoes more treacherous.

The El Niño of '97

1997 was one of the worst El Niño years ever. Massive flooding and huge mudslides hit Peru. Drought in Indonesia caused forest fires that burned for months. In East Africa, torrential rainfall ruined crops. And unusually, terrible **twisters** struck the US state of Florida.

During the last 50 years, El Niño features have appeared 31 per cent of the time, and La Niña 23 per cent. This means that stable conditions occurred only 46 per cent of the time.

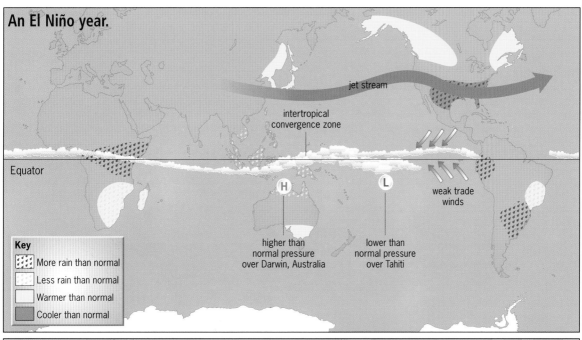

An El Niño year.

jet stream

intertropical convergence zone

Equator

H

L

weak trade winds

higher than normal pressure over Darwin, Australia

lower than normal pressure over Tahiti

Key

More rain than normal
Less rain than normal
Warmer than normal
Cooler than normal

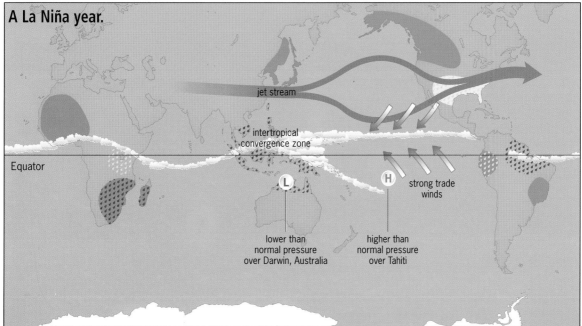

A La Niña year.

jet stream

intertropical convergence zone

Equator

L

H

strong trade winds

lower than normal pressure over Darwin, Australia

higher than normal pressure over Tahiti

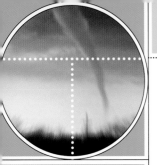

Measuring tornadoes

The **Fujita-Pearson scale** is a measurement of the amount of damage done by a particular tornado. The scale was developed by Professor Fujita, and Allen Pearson, the director of the US National Severe Storm Forecast Laboratory, in 1971. The scale shows how fast the tornado spins and also gives an idea of the type of damage and severity of damage for each strength. As well as this it also divides the length of the **path** into three categories: short, intermediate and long.

Australia also uses the Fujita-Pearson scale, but many other countries measure their tornadoes on the Tornado Intensity Scale (TIS). This is also called the TORRO scale and is used by the British Tornado and Storm Research Organization. TIS is again based on damage. On the TIS scale, a T10–11 is called a super-tornado. The worst tornadoes in Britain have reached T8 on the scale, which is rated as severely devastating.

A tornado sometimes seems to skip along. This means that it might pick up a whole building lying in its path, but then leave intact the next one straight in front of it.

Fujita-Pearson scale

Category of tornado	Speed of rotation		Damage done
	kilometres per hour	miles per hour	
F0 (weak)	less than 116	less than 72	Branches broken off trees; some damage to chimneys; pushes over shallow rooted plants; knocks over sign boards.
F1 (weak)	117–180	73–112	Mobile homes blown sideways, or blown over; moving cars blown off roads; peels surface – eg: tiles, shingles, thatch – off roofs.
F2 (strong)	181–253	113–157	Complete roofs torn off frame houses; mobile homes demolished; large trees uprooted or snapped; light objects eg: fence posts, garden canes turned into flying missiles.
F3 (strong)	254–331	158–206	Roofs and some walls torn off well constructed houses; most trees in forests uprooted; trains overturned.
F4 (violent)	332–418	207–260	Well constructed houses flattened; cars thrown and large objects turned into flying missiles.
F5 (violent)	419–512	261–318	Strong frame houses can be lifted off foundations and carried considerable distances; car sized missiles fly through the air and can be carried more than 100 metres; steel reinforced concrete structures, eg: bridges, badly damaged.

The path	
Short path	up to 0.5 kilometres (0.3 miles) long
Intermediate path	5.3–51.4 kilometres (3.3–31.9 miles) long
Long path	51.5 kilometres (32.0 miles) long or more

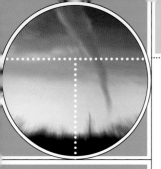

Storm-chasers

Tornadoes are terrifying but they are also fascinating. They draw the attention of scientists and members of the public alike.

Storm-chasing – why do they do it?

In the United States, storm-chasing is a hobby. The amazing sight of an uncontrollable, furious tornado whirling across America's vast and beautiful landscapes is an attraction that some people just cannot resist. Since the action film *Twister*, more people have taken to storm-chasing but they have not necessarily taken the trouble to read about tornadoes and take the right safety precautions.

Serious spotters are experienced amateur storm-chasers who watch **tornadigenic** thunder clouds and track any tornadoes that emerge from them. They carry with them digital phones, two-way radios or fax machines to warn the National Weather Service when they believe a serious tornado is forming. Many are members of America's Amateur Radio Service, which works closely with National Weather Service Field Officers – the **meteorologists**. Often, their observations are vital, as even **radar** cannot track **touchdown** at certain angles.

These storm-chasers are often the first on the scene after a tornado has struck. They are also trained in first aid and carry a good first aid kit. They can use these to help people suffering from heart attacks due to shock, those struck by lightning, or hit by flooding or the tornado itself. Detailed maps show these spotters where they can escape a **funnel** by moving quickly onto side roads.

Make your own tornado!

A simple spinning, **vortex** effect can be made by using just two plastic bottles, some water and some sticky tape. First, fill one of the plastic bottles with water. Then, turn the empty bottle upside-down and tape the necks of both bottles together. Now turn the bottles over so that the one with water in it is on top, and watch the vortex form as the water flows down into the empty bottle.

Untrained spotters can get caught in the severe rain that often hits before the tornado strikes. Without detailed maps they do not know how to escape from narrow, badly-made country roads which easily get flooded.

Some spotters follow the tornado to catch it on film or photographs, which they can then sell to newspapers and TV networks. TV stations often sponsor storm-chasers to do this. They also send up helicopters with film crews.

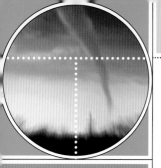

Tracking tornadoes

It is very difficult to predict where a tornado will begin and where it will end up. Experienced storm-watchers know that deep thunderclouds with dark bulges underneath are a sign that tornadoes might be forming. This is because each bulge is a small lump of circulating air and **water vapour** – a **supercell** – that can give rise to a spinning **twister**.

As the tornado approaches, it gives out a strange smell, rather like sulphur or strong seaweed. This is **ozone**, a gas normally found high up in the **atmosphere**. The last warning is a loud hissing, whistling or roaring sound. What this noise means is that it is too late to get out of the way. Hopefully, most people will be hearing the sound of the tornado from a safe place but this depends on warnings based on accurate measurements of an approaching twister.

Damage done to buildings and trees by flying debris gives scientists an idea of how fast a tornado is travelling.

Radar readings

For over 20 years, in the United States, tornadoes have been quite successfully tracked using the **Doppler radar** system. The radar station sends out microwave pulses which bounce off **super-cooled** raindrops or ice crystals inside the cloud. The signal which bounces back to the radar station shows the movement in the cloud. When a hook-shaped signal shows up, it means that a circular movement of wind is about to move out – and the tornado will form.

Radar is especially important for tracking tornadoes that cannot easily be spotted, for example at night or when they are wrapped in cloud or torrential rain. The Doppler system enables weather stations to give a 25-minute warning, which is enough time for people to find proper shelter. However, the system is not perfect. Not all tornadoes emerge from the hook – some form completely unnoticed.

Tornado tremors

As the tornado approaches, its sucking movement creates vibrations in the ground. Scientists are creating a detection device to measure the strength of the ground's tremors as the twister moves. It is based on the **seismometer**, which is the instrument used for measuring earthquakes.

This instrument is known as a **TOTO**. TOTOs are placed along the tornado track, and use Doppler radar and other instruments to make measurements inside the tornado as the **funnel** passes right over them.

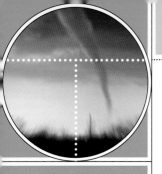

Touchdown!

Not every tornado touches down but, when it does, it carves out a very visible **path** of devastation. This path may be as short as a few kilometres or it might run on for 750 kilometres (about 470 miles). The sucking **funnel** itself may be quite narrow – no more than 100 metres (about 330 feet) at its widest point – or it may be as wide as 1.5 kilometres (about 1 mile).

The tornado's path is sometimes clearly marked and the damage is confined to a neatly-edged strip. At other times, the edges are jagged, where high winds have thrown flying debris from the tornado's track into standing objects. In this case, the visible path can be many times wider than the width of the funnel itself. People are usually killed by collapsed buildings, by flying debris or by being picked up by the **twister** and thrown back down to the ground again.

Tornado facts

Damage is caused by four processes.

- Wind pressure: this can reach several hundreds of kilograms per square metre (hundreds of pounds per square foot). This is like being hit by a high-speed train. It is a combination of the rotating speed and the forward motion.

- Wind speed and suction within the funnel: this is strong enough to lift roofs, walls and even whole buildings.

- The conflict between the extremely **low pressure** inside the funnel and the **high pressure** within a building: this can actually cause doors, windows and even walls to blow out.

- Twisting action: when sucking, thrusting winds are greater on one side of a tree than the other, then the tops of trees can get twisted off.

Comparing the damage

On the **Fujita-Pearson** tornado scale, F3 is called a strong twister. It is a very common tornado strength in the United States. It can severely damage a wooden structure. The huge number of wooden buildings in the United States makes tornado damage far worse than in some other countries where most buildings are made of brick, stone or concrete. In Britain, for example, the same amount of destruction would take stronger rotating and forward-moving winds than those of an F3. This is because so many of Britain's buildings are made of brick or stone.

An F5 tornado on the Fujita scale is strong enough to rip up paving stones from walkways, and concrete or tar from road surfaces.

The worst twister disaster the United States has ever experienced began in the state of Missouri on 18 March 1925. A total of seven tornadoes flattened a path 700 kilometres (435 miles) long and 1.5 kilometres (about 1 mile) wide through Indiana and Illinois. They left hundreds of thousands homeless and 695 people died. This house in Indiana was picked up and dropped 18 metres (50 feet) from its foundations!

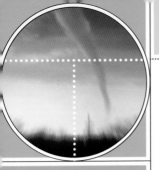

Preventing the damage

Early warning

Nothing can prevent tornadoes from damaging buildings and vehicles and ripping up crops. Well-rehearsed **evacuation** into proper tornado shelters is the best way to avoid death and injury. This relies on accurate predictions that are linked to widely broadcast warning systems. As we saw on page 31, **Doppler radar** has enabled people to be evacuated much earlier. It is quite accurate, too, detecting 94 per cent of all damaging tornadoes. Before this, the rate was only 64 per cent.

Televised warnings

Experienced amateur tornado-watchers will be looking closely at their television screens when they see rolling thunderclouds in the distance. This is because the lightning in **tornadigenic cloud** (tornado-forming cloud) produces interference with radio signals, making the television screen brighter. This interference is known as **spherics** and can help to detect tornadoes up to about 20 kilometres (12 miles) away.

Early warnings can be provided by Doppler radar, and by storm-chasers who are watching tornadigenic thunderstorms for signs of tornado formation.

Where can you hide?

Using all the scientific evidence, most weather stations can issue only a 25-minute warning for a severe tornado. In the United States these are given over the radio, on the television and the Internet. Emergency vehicles like police cars give advice over loudspeakers.

At home, most people shut themselves in a concrete tornado shelter, a reinforced closet or a basement. The north-east side of a building is considered the safest place, as most tornadoes in the US whirl their way from the south-west, hitting the south-west corner of a building first.

Public tornado shelters and subways are used by people who are out on the streets when a tornado strikes. Many tornadoes seem to occur in the late afternoon and early evening, often when crowds of workers are making their way home.

Making it safe

After a reconstruction of tornado damage experienced during the Wichita Falls disaster, scientists at Texas Technical University have designed tornado shelters that can be built in the home. To test them, they shoot large wooden poles into the shelter walls to try out the strength. Wind tunnels are used to simulate tornadoes and the kind of damage that can be done by tornadoes of different strengths. This helps scientists and authorities to set up accurate building regulations for constructing homes, offices and tornado shelters.

Despite all the warnings and advice, there are still unnecessary deaths from tornadoes. It is clear that there is still a lot that needs to be done to persuade people to take notice of planning regulations and warning systems.

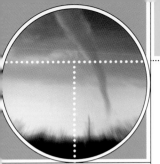

Why live in the path of tornadoes?

It is difficult to know exactly when and where a tornado will strike, so planning to live out of their way is impossible. In the United States, **Tornado Alley** cuts across some of the best farming country. Some very large cities are there, too. In Britain, tornadoes usually spread up from the south coast. As they move northwards they, too, pass through prime agricultural land, and it is in the southern part of the country that the population is most concentrated. However, tornadoes in Britain can strike the northern, more remote part of the islands too.

For the people of Bangladesh, there is no alternative to living in the danger zones. The **twisters' paths** cut across the most densely populated part of the country, where people have to farm and fish in order to survive. Tornadoes usually occur here at the same time as devastating **hurricanes** and fearsome floods.

These soldiers are helping residents in Midwest City, Oklahoma after the May 1999 tornado. Armed forces can help with the rescue and protect homes and businesses from looting.

What have we learned?

People still come to live in areas prone to tornadoes. Perhaps they feel secure because scientists have developed so many ways of monitoring tornadoes. There is plenty of advice on building strong shelters and hiding from the storm, too.

Sadly, in Oklahoma on the evening of 3 May 1999, none of this prevented 45 deaths, many injuries and utter devastation. The highest-ever recorded wind raged at the centre of the **vortex** of the main tornado, reaching 512 kilometres per hour (320 miles per hour). The main **funnel** was a mass of vortices that merged together over just six hours. It ripped apart communities and suburbs on the edge of Oklahoma City. Even brick-built buildings were torn apart. As usual, though, it was wooden structures and trailers (mobile homes) that were worst hit.

It seems that until more is done to change the type of buildings that lie in the path of tornadoes, disaster will strike time and again. Added to this, many people in Tornado Alley still do not take tornado warnings seriously enough. In Oklahoma on 3 May 1999, motorists were still driving along the highway even though they knew that a tornado was just ten minutes away!

When a tornado strikes people often need to be rescued from under debris. This man has been freed by emergency workers following the August 1999 tornado in Salt Lake City in the United States.

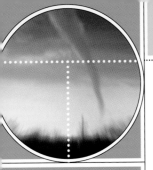

Tornadoes and nature

'The cougars have gone into their shelters. But the deer have just come out, so things are looking okay.' These were the confident words of Gary Harp as he looked out onto the miniature zoo in his back garden. This was on Tuesday 4 May 1999, in Hope Township, in the south-east corner of Oklahoma State. His animals were right. The long, persistent storm warnings of the previous hours and days were false alarms. The tornadoes brewing in the huge bank of clouds making its way through the state missed Hope Township and headed straight for Oklahoma City.

Many creatures seem to sense the oncoming **twister** but no one really knows why. It could be the change in air pressure or distant vibrations but, when the tornado strikes, nature suffers as well as human beings. Animals, including pigs, sheep and even cows and horses are sucked up and thrown aside, plant life is flattened and torn up and massive trees are twisted, snapped or uprooted.

Animal tragedies

There are well-documented modern examples of **waterspouts** sucking up fish, water plants and even alligators and throwing them ashore. Over hundreds of years there have been showers of dried peas, hazelnuts and other plants. Crabs, winkles, starfish, eels and frogs have also rained down – all far from any water mass. This leads us to believe that tornadoes and waterspouts are capable of sucking up creatures, carrying them in the air and then setting or throwing them down elsewhere. Usually, the tornado sucks up creatures and then drops them straight down again. However, if they are drawn up to a great height it is possible that the continuing strong, upward motion of warm air can keep them aloft for huge distances.

A natural disaster

On 20 July 1662, a tornado struck Cheshire, a county in the north of England. This is a description of the effect it had upon the plants and animals lying in its way.

...in the forest of Maxfield (Macclesfield) *there arose a great pillar of smoke, in height like a steeple, and judged twenty yards* (18 metres) *abroad, which making the most hideous noise, went along the ground six or seven miles* (10–11 kilometres), *levelling all the way... The terrible noise it made so frightened the cattle, that they ran away, and were thereby preserved; it passed over a cornfield, and laid it as low with the ground as if it had been trodden down by feet; it went through a wood, and turned up above an hundred trees by the roots; coming into a field full of cocks of hay ready to be carried in, it swept all away so that scarce a handful of it could be found, only it left a great tree in the middle of the field, which it had brought from some other place.*

On 31 August 1997 in Nottinghamshire, England, a tornado sucked up 40 pig huts and threw them 30 metres (100 ft) into the air. The pigs were tossed almost a kilometre (about half a mile) from their homes. A boy reported seeing some flying around chimney pots. Sadly, most of them died when they hit the ground.

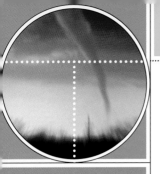

Tornado tales

The list of fantastic **twister** tales is almost endless. Some are frightening, while others are simply incredible – but true.

Strange stories in Floyds Knobs

On 2 June 1990 a tornado struck Floyds Knobs, a town in Indiana, in the United States. The twister hurtled through the town during the night and when people awoke they exchanged some very strange tales indeed. One family heard a loud noise, like a diving aeroplane, and hid in the bathroom. All, that is, except their eight-year-old son, who was sucked up by the tornado and set down some 90 metres (300 feet) from the house. In the morning, the house was just a pile of sticks – and a bathroom. The family emerged safely and found their son lying unharmed in a nearby field. Other families had similar tales to tell, but perhaps the luckiest resident of Floyds Knobs was a cow, which was discovered stuck in a tree, mooing crossly.

Tornado facts

- In 1987 in Cerney Wick, England, small pink frogs showered down on the village.

- Tyres, empty oil drums, tin cans and, sadly, birds, have all been sucked up and exploded in a tornado.

- In a tornado birds' feathers are sucked off their bodies, leaving them completely plucked.

- Flowers, stalks and leaves have been embedded deep in the wood of tree trunks.

- A house in Oklahoma was sucked up, twisted around through 90° and then set down again.

Miracle baby

In Oklahoma on 3 May 1999, a one-year-old baby girl was ripped from a bathroom where her family was sheltering, and blown away. Her parents were severely injured. Her grandmother lay dying and her grandfather thought that the baby could not possibly have survived, but a police sheriff found her lying in the mud by the base of a tree some distance from her home. She had some small cuts and bruises but otherwise was fine.

Nutty tornadoes

On 12 February 1979 six showers of mustard and cress seed fell on a glass conservatory in Southampton, England. The man inside realized only later that his garden was covered with the seeds. Nearby, other people had similar experiences over the next few days as they were showered with peas, maize and haricot beans. No one knew where they came from, but a young boy said that he had seen seeds pouring out of a small black cloud. There are very few possible explanations for these phenomena, except for tornado activity.

Small nuts and seeds are easily sucked up and carried by a tornado.

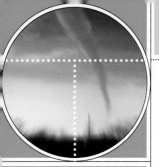

Tornadoes in history

After the Oklahoma tornado disaster of 3 May 1999, one of its victims said, 'It was like a devil black cloud.' Long ago, people really did believe that tornadoes were evil spirits – devils – punishing people for their wicked ways. No one knew then how tornadoes were formed, or even that they were associated with the weather. The following extract comes from the first written account of a tornado, which occurred in County Westmeath, Ireland, in CE1055.

> *...a great steeple of fire, in the exact shape of a circular belfry, or what we now call a round tower. For nine hours it remained there in sight of all: and during the whole time, flocks of large dark-coloured birds ... kept flying in and out through the door and windows... Sometimes a great number of them would swoop suddenly down, and snatch up in their long talons dogs, cats or any other small animal that happened to lie in their way; and when they had risen again to a great height they would drop them dead to the ground.*

The 'birds' were debris being sucked up and tossed around, but no one knew this at the time. Descriptions like these occurred well into the seventeenth century. By the end of it, though, greater scientific knowledge enabled witnesses to link tornadoes with certain weather conditions. The following observation was made when a **whirlwind** spun through Yorkshire, England, in 1687.

> *...the wind thus blowing soon created a great **vortex**, **gyrating** and whirling amongst the clouds; the centre of which every now and then dropt down in the shape of a thick long black pipe, commonly called a spout, in which I could distinctly view a motion like that of a screw...*

Fear in France

Tornadoes are common features in much of Europe, especially Britain, Russia, Italy and France. France has seen some of the widest and longest **paths** in Europe, and the earliest tornado recorded in France is also Europe's longest so far observed. It occurred in September 1669, and overnight swept a 400-kilometre (250-mile) track from La Rochelle in the south to Paris in the north. Some scientists believe it began further south as a **waterspout** in the Bay of Biscay, but we have to be careful about very early recordings of tornadoes. The only instrument available for observing them at that time was the telescope.

This is Valetta Harbour in Malta. One of the earliest recorded waterspouts whirled into the harbour some time in the 1550s. It smashed a fleet of ships, killing about 600 sailors who were about to set sail for battle.

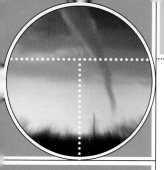

Amazing tornadoes

Ten deadly tornadoes

These are ten of the most deadly tornado and waterspout disasters recorded. The tornado disasters were mostly the result of more than a single **funnel** and **touchdown**.

Date	Place	Cause	No. of deaths
2 April 1977	Bangladesh	Tornadoes	900
18 March 1925	United States	Tornado	689
23 September 1551 or 1556	Valetta, Malta	Waterspout	600
December 1851	Sicily, Italy	Tornadoes	500
9 June 1984	Western Russia	Tornado	400
3 April 1974	USA and Canada	Tornadoes	315
11 April 1965	United States	Tornadoes	271
19 August 1845	Montville, France	Tornado	200
February 1971	United States	Tornadoes	115
9 June 1953	United States	Tornado	94

Whirlwinds (left) can be almost as spectacular as tornadoes (right). On the salt flats of Utah, United States, a whirlwind 750 metres (about 2500 feet) high was spotted whipping up salt dust. It travelled for over 60 kilometres (nearly 40 miles) and lasted seven hours.

Tornado facts

- The United States is hit by between 600 and 1000 tornadoes every year. Over half of these occur in spring, more than a quarter in summer and the rest in autumn and winter.

- More than 80 per cent of tornadoes occur between midday and midnight, with more than 20 per cent between 4 p.m. and 6 p.m. This is because more thunderclouds gather during the afternoon, due to the warmth.

- The largest tornado outbreak in Europe occurred in Britain on 21 November 1981. In just over five hours, 105 tornadoes struck from Wales in the west to Humberside in the north-east. The strongest was T5 – but no one was killed.

Glossary

altitude the height of something above sea level, especially atmosphere

atmosphere bands of gases high up that are wrapped around the earth

ball lightning a type of lightning that is shaped like a ball and can last for much longer than normal lightning

carbon gases gases formed by burning fossil fuels such as coal and oil

climate the general weather type and conditions

communications facilities like roads, railways and telephone lines

condense when water or other vapour turns back into liquid

convection current movements of cold and warm air that are then spun into a vortex

cumulonimbus a type of cloud which is very dense and contains a lot of water vapour. Cumulonimbus clouds often contain thunderstorms and strong updraughts and downdraughts.

depression an area of very low air pressure

Doppler dome a tough, dome-shaped building housing Doppler radar and other instruments for measuring tornadoes as they whirl over it

Doppler radar an instrument which measures radio waves reflected off water droplets or ice particles in thunderclouds – the change in frequency as the droplets move shows the shape of movement made by the droplets; it can reveal the hook-shape of a forming tornado

dust devil a whirling wind that whips up dust and debris, rather like a tornado – but it begins from the ground and is fed by warm air radiating from it (also known as a whirlwind)

electrical charge a build up of electricity, which is either positive or negative, like static

El Niño the effect of changing wind directions and warm ocean currents on the climate, and on climatic features such as tornadoes and hurricanes

evacuate to move people to safety

evaporate to change from a liquid into a gas

eye the calm centre inside the hurricane where the skies are clear – but it is surrounded by the swirling cloud and winds in the hurricane walls

front a front is where two air masses meet – one is cold and one is warm

Fujita-Pearson scale a scale invented by Professor Fujita and Allen Pearson which is used to measure the strength of tornadoes

funnel the twisting 'snout' or tube of tornado cloud

global warming the rise in the Earth's temperature – possibly due to the emission of carbon gases – possibly due to flares from the Sun

greenhouse effect when carbon gases are released into the atmosphere, reflecting heat back onto Earth

gyrate to spin and twist

high pressure where a cool, dry air mass is descending the pressure of the air will be high

humid air which is carrying a lot of water vapour

hurricane a wide, revolving storm with winds that blow at over 110 kilometres per hour (75 miles per hour) – it forms in a similar way to a tornado but on a much larger scale

instability see 'unstable' below

jet stream   a very strong, narrow westerly wind that blows high up – about 10 000 metres (30 000 feet) high

La Niña   the reversal of the action on the climate of the El Niño effect (see above) – winds blowing from the east are weaker, those from the west, stronger

low pressure   where a warm air mass is rising the pressure of the air will be low

meteorologists   scientists who study climate and weather

methane   a gas formed from decaying plant matter

ozone   a layer of protective gases 10–50 kilometres (6–30 miles) above the Earth

ozone hole   a huge, thin patch in the atmosphere where ozone gases should be

path   the track, and the length of the track, taken by the tornado

prevailing winds   a wind that blows continually in one direction

radar   high-powered pulses of radio reflected off objects to give an idea of their position and shape

radiate   to send out rays of light, heat or other energy

radiation   when the Sun's heat rays hit the Earth and the heat is reflected back

seismometer   instrument for measuring vibrations in the Earth – often an early signal of tornado movement across the ground

spherics   interference with radio signals (atmospherics)

stratosphere   the layer of atmosphere (band of gases) just above the troposphere (see below)

supercell   a small lump of circulating air and water vapour within a thundercloud – one of the first signs of a tornado

super-cooled   water can be cooled to below freezing when it is in droplet form in a cloud. If it touches something else, even a dust or ice particle, it immediately freezes, and forms hail.

tornadigenic (cloud)   cloud that is likely to form tornadoes

Tornado Alley   the stretch of the United States in which tornadoes commonly strike – it runs from the Gulf of Mexico to the Great Lakes in the north

TOTO   an instrument housing Doppler radar equipment for measuring wind speeds and directions inside the tornado

touchdown   when a tornado funnel hits the ground

troposphere   the layer of atmosphere (band of gases) closest to the earth

turbulence/turbulent   if air is forced to rise or descend rapidly it forms eddies and choppy waves, just like in a stream when water is forced around a rock

twister   another name for a tornado, particularly used in the United States

unstable   when air is stable it is dry and cool. When it is unstable it is the opposite – warm, moist and likely to make clouds, rain and even storms.

ultra-violet rays   light outside the range of visible wavelengths, which comes from the Sun

vacuum   a space without any air or particles in it, like in space

volcanic   to do with volcanoes

vortex   (more than one = vortices) the twisting funnel of a tornado

water cycle   the way in which the Earth's supply of water is recycled in different forms – as water vapour, rain, snow, sleet, hail or ice

water vapour   water in its gaseous state – it has been heated so the water molecules expand and change into a gas

waterspout   a tornado formation over water – the water, mist and spray are sucked up, twisted around and showered around the base of the vortex

whirlwind   see 'dust devil' above

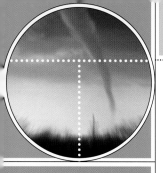

Index